VINTAGE
LOUISIANA SIGNS

We might as well welcome you to this retrospective of Louisiana's vintage signage with the sight that greeted travelers as they entered the state on major highways. This card was postmarked in Tallulah in May 1957, and the message on the back reads, "On our way to Natchez now! Down the Mississippi in a Dodge—That ain't easy to do!"

VINTAGE

LOUISIANA SIGNS

TIM HOLLIS

THE
History
PRESS

Published by The History Press
Charleston, SC
www.historypress.com

First published 2025

Manufactured in China

ISBN 9781467156943

Library of Congress Control Number 2024945980.

THIS PAGE Photos of the Mardi Gras celebration in New Orleans usually managed to capture much of the flavor of the city's downtown signage in the background. In the top photo, to the left of Rhealee Millinery, the Woolworth's store seems to be undergoing some remodeling. In the bottom shot, we see a furrier's vertical sign that appears to feature a leopard—no doubt the source of some of the furs they sold.

The Oaks Motel sign in Opelousas illustrates the fate so common to its roadside brethren. The motel was razed around 2014, but the sign kept a lonely vigil for several more years, with its yellow neon tubing slowly crumbling. *Debra Jane Seltzer collection.*

CONTENTS

THIS PAGE Probably no other part of Louisiana had its signage documented in as many different photos and postcards as New Orleans's Canal Street. Even photos taken from approximately the same angle but only a few years apart can show great changes. These two make a great primer on the subject; we will see more of Canal in multiple chapters to come. The top photo gives a glimpse of the Loews State movie palace on the right and the Krauss department store on the left; in the lower part of the bottom photo, we can see the result of the Woolworth's remodeling from the Mardi Gras shot on page 5. Both, of course, prominently show the Marriott Hotel and the "Jet Delta" sign.

ACKNOWLEDGEMENTS

Although much of the material you will see in the pages that follow originated in my own decades-long collection of memorabilia, kudos must be given to the additional sources that enlivened the result. As you will notice in the credit lines for the photos, a number of them (as well as other helpful information) came from fellow tourism collectors, historians and photographers: Holly Aguirre, Al Coleman, Ted Perry, Donnie Pitchford, Debra Jane Seltzer and Stephanie Stuckey.

We must also acknowledge the late photographer John Margolies, who bequeathed his personal archive to the Library of Congress with the amazing stipulation that no restrictions were to be imposed on its use by other authors and researchers.

The author (left, in case you couldn't tell) meets legendary animator/director Chuck Jones during an exhibit at the Carolyn Summers Gallery, 312 Royal Street in the French Quarter, February 18, 1984.

INTRODUCTION

This volume in our "Vintage Signs" series is a little different than the previous installments concerning Alabama, Tennessee and Georgia. My own personal experience with Louisiana, unlike those three states, is rather limited—but it has been a fascinating journey to pull together all the materials and the stories behind them from so many different sources.

Our first family visit to the state was in July 1969, a couple of months before I started first grade. My mom and dad and I made what was, for us anyway, quite a sweep along the Gulf Coast, taking in New Orleans and the Mississippi beaches and ending up in Mobile, Alabama, the night the astronauts landed on the moon. (They had to land at night, you see, because the moon wouldn't have been out during the day.) The strangest aspect of that whole trip is that, other than a few color shots taken in Mobile at the end, we had no photographic documentation of it at all. I have to believe that my dad's trusty old 35 mm camera somehow malfunctioned and caused an entire roll of film to be undeveloped. Had our photos from Biloxi and Gulfport come out unscathed, they would have been priceless documentation of that area shortly before Hurricane Camille wiped the slate clean later that fall.

We did keep brochures and postcards and a few souvenirs of that trip, but of the New Orleans leg of the journey I remember absolutely nothing. Apparently there was little in that historical city to make an impression on a six-year-old, as even having those small bits of documentation does not spark any memories.

Believe it or not, it took from first grade until my senior year of college before I returned to Louisiana. Through a circuitous route I won't go into right now, I received an invitation to an art exhibit in New Orleans honoring the great animation director Chuck Jones (of Looney Tunes and *How the Grinch Stole Christmas!* fame, among many other credits). The presentation was taking place at a gallery in the French Quarter in February 1984, and the sheer pandemonium of trying to get there and find a parking space with the beginnings of Mardi Gras going on rather precluded taking many photos. However, in our chapter on motels, you will see a most historic photo I took in Slidell on that trip, so just stay tuned for that.

Enough background info (or non-info, as the case may be). *Vintage Louisiana Signs* follows the general pattern set by the previous volumes in the series, devoting chapters to shopping, food, automotive businesses, tourist attractions (where Louisiana really fell behind its fellow southern states) and amusement places. Be aware that it is not a comprehensive overview of any of these topics; there were many other notable signs that might have been included, but photographic documentation of them was either nonexistent or unavailable for publication. When given a choice, most of the signs to be found here are ones that no longer exist, although a few present-day landmarks will be found to seep through every now and then.

One last, and similar, thought: in no way should this book be considered the final word on Louisiana's vintage signage. In fact, during the months it was being assembled, there were news stories about the discovery and/or preservation of several landmark New Orleans signs that did not even make it into the book, including the Dew Drop Inn, McKenzie's Bakery and the painted wall sign at the Beachcorner bar. So the story is going to be continuing into the future—and we will all just have to wait to see how it is documented by others in years to come.

CHAPTER ONE

STORE SIGNS AND ROTO-SPHERES

Our first chapter looks at the many different types of signage associated with shopping and other retail, so naturally we find ourselves back on Canal Street, but this time for an incredible nighttime shot. Obviously two of the most prominent signs are for those fondly remembered department stores Holmes and Godchaux's, but if you examine this photo closely, you'll see more additional retailers and their signs than could ever be itemized here—even including billboards for a couple of different brands of liquor.

Ryan Street, Lake Charles, La.

OPPOSITE, TOP Small towns had their "downtown" shopping districts too. This 1936 view of Leesville shows not only the hotel and the traditional corner drugstore but also a location of the Morgan and Lindsey five-and-ten chain based in Texas.

OPPOSITE, BOTTOM Meanwhile, over in Alexandria, Wellan's was the homegrown department store of choice. This colorful view dates from 1959, and at the far right-hand edge we can see that chain department stores, in this case JCPenney, were beginning to horn in on such local retailers' formerly undisputed territory.

ABOVE Now we're in Lake Charles, where most of the signs somewhat blend together due to the rather primitive "colorization" methods used by the postcard company. Besides Goodrich Tires and, in the far distance, the tall marquee for the Paramount Theater, the most prominent sign is for the Charleston Hotel. While the theater's site is now a parking lot, the hotel still proudly serves guests to this day.

OPPOSITE, TOP This view looking down Lake Charles's Ryan Street from the opposite direction was postmarked in 1961, although the photo could be from a little earlier. Now retail giants Woolworth's and Sears dominate the scenery, but look closely and you may also be able to spy, with your little eye, a more localized store known as The Fair.

OPPOSITE, BOTTOM By now it should be obvious that pretty much every town had its own locally based department store, and in Shreveport, it was Feibleman's that had the honor. This view of main drag Texas Street looking east dates from 1937.

ABOVE By the time of this view of Texas Street looking west, Feibleman's had gone to wherever old department stores go when they die and had become Shreveport's Sears location (the green vertical sign in the background). Closer to the camera, we again meet our old buddy Woolworth's, with the neon Walgreens sign halfway between. And we must not forget that lighted cross atop the First Methodist Church at the far end of the street.

Louisiana department stores didn't get much more legendary than New Orleans's Maison Blanche. In 1947, the store introduced Santa's assistant Mr. Bingle (who just happened to share the same initials). He was so successful that Maison Blanche's parent company, City Stores of New Jersey, farmed out the roly-poly snowman to several of its other chains, including Lowenstein's in Memphis and Loveman's in Birmingham.

Mardi Gras Float from the Realms of Phantasy

TOP Several pages ago, we mentioned that Mardi Gras photos were dependable sources for documenting New Orleans signage, and here is yet another one. Among the many stores captured in this angle is Rubensteins Men's Clothing, which, unlike so many others we have seen, is still doing business in the same location today.

BOTTOM The S.H. Kress variety stores were well known for their magnificent architecture, and the one on Canal Street was a prime example. Like many of the others, its built-in Kress signage was left in place even after it was adapted into other usage—in its case, it was combined with the adjacent Maison Blanche to become today's Ritz-Carlton Hotel. *Debra Jane Seltzer collection.*

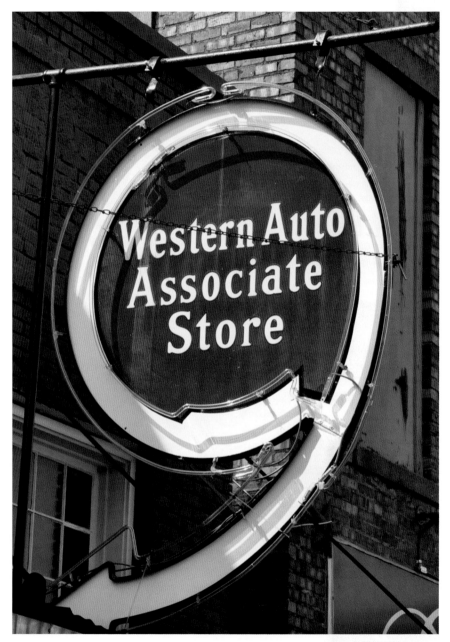

Western Auto was hardly in the same league as Maison Blanche, but these circular arrow signs were familiar sights on small-town Main Streets from coast to coast. This survivor, with neon still intact, could be seen in Minden a few years ago. *Debra Jane Seltzer collection.*

THIS PAGE Have you ever seen one of these shapes on a business's sign and wondered what it was? Some people referred to them as Sputniks, but their actual name was Roto-Spheres, and they were invented by Bossier City signmaker Warren Milks. Not only did the globe revolve atop its pole, but the two halves also rotated, giving a constantly changing view of the sixteen multicolored neon spikes. This is a restored 1960 Roto-Sphere that was displayed for a while at a Shreveport sign company's offices. *Both, Debra Jane Seltzer collection.*

ABOVE Mel's Diner in Broussard displayed this re-creation of a Roto-Sphere that had only ten neon spikes instead of the usual sixteen. It also did not rotate, but it brought back fond memories for most people who would not notice those details. *Debra Jane Seltzer collection.*

OPPOSITE For sheer neon euphoria, even the Roto-Spheres had to bow their heads to the Walgreens drugstore on Canal Street in New Orleans. Although it now uses LED lighting rather than neon, the store has meticulously retained the original look from when it was built in 1938. *Both, Stephanie Stuckey collection.*

ABOVE Most drugstores, of course, did not expend nearly as much effort and expense on their signage as the New Orleans Walgreens. However, that did not mean they could not have their own appeal. This store in Shreveport likely shared the expense for this appealing sign with Coca-Cola to advertise its soda fountain. *John Margolies collection.*

OPPOSITE Here's another version of a drugstore sign, this time a three-dimensional rendition of the mortar and pestle, traditional emblem of the retail pharmacy. And as a bonus, notice another extinct species just below it: the sign for a pay telephone. Both symbols of the past, for sure. *John Margolies collection.*

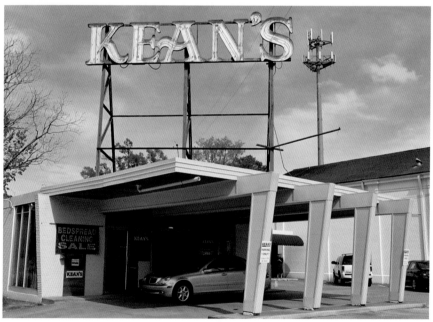

OPPOSITE, TOP This vintage Kelvinator sign—which hung over a long-closed dealer in Abbeville—serves to get us away from drugstores and into other types of businesses that were centered on appliances. Sort of. That was the best transition we could think up, so give us a break, willya? *Debra Jane Seltzer collection.*

OPPOSITE, BOTTOM The chain of Kean's dry cleaners has been cleaning up in Baton Rouge for well over a century. This location, with its tall rooftop sign, eventually became a Crispy Catch seafood restaurant and helped customers add grease to their clothes that could be removed at other Kean's outlets. *Debra Jane Seltzer collection.*

ABOVE Just what is the difference between a washateria and a laundromat? If you find out, let us know. Between places such as this one and the many Kean's locations, Baton Rouge must have had the cleanest clothes in Louisiana. *Debra Jane Seltzer collection.*

ABOVE Another cleaners chain with locations in several towns was White Star. This one in Houma supplemented its neon star with a close relative of the Roto-Sphere mounted above. *Debra Jane Seltzer collection.*

OPPOSITE Here's a closer look at another of the not-a-Roto-Sphere "satellite" balls in Monroe. Notice that it uses clear light bulbs instead of the Roto-Sphere's multicolored neon projectiles. *Debra Jane Seltzer collection.*

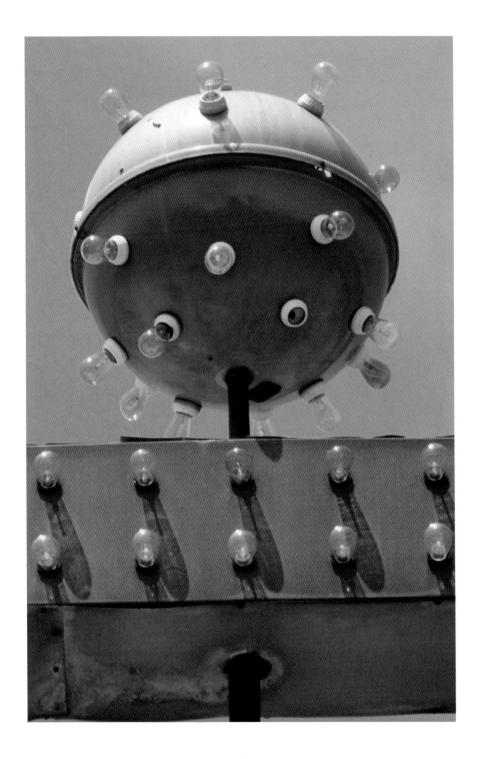

One of the most fondly remembered brands of children's shoes is Red Goose—mainly for its many promotions, including "Reddy Goose" comic books and the goose statue that would lay a golden egg with a prize inside. This Red Goose sign in Thibodaux later served as the emblem of a bar of the same name. *Debra Jane Seltzer collection.*

RIGHT For those who preferred a pair of cowboy boots over Red Goose shoes, there was Topps Western World, which still sells cowboy duds to would-be western dudes in Bossier City. This giant John Wayne is still on duty too, at a companion business known as Topps Trailer Sales. *John Margolies collection.*

BELOW What does an airplane about to crash into a building have to do with a store that sells beds and bedding supplies? It certainly does not inspire visions of peaceful slumber, that's for sure, but in the world of roadside signage, it didn't have to make sense as long as it got passersby to stop and shop for a while. *John Margolies collection.*

OPPOSITE The building that housed this now-defunct printing plant in Lafayette has a history even more notable than its sign. It was originally the headquarters for Hadacol, a purported tonic that included a high percentage of alcohol content and later inspired the ageless *I Love Lucy* product Vitameatavegamin. *Debra Jane Seltzer collection.*

RIGHT We can't help wondering if this neon obelisk outside a bank in Leesville was meant to evoke visions of the Washington Monument. After all, there were a lot of George Washingtons housed inside. *Debra Jane Seltzer collection.*

LEFT It's quite unusual for a bank to advertise with its own cartoon mascot, and even more unusual for a small hometown bank to do it, but Winnfield First Federal came up with "Winni the First" in the early 1970s. He was used heavily in newspaper ads and presumably would have appeared on signage around the financial institution as well. This amazingly detailed vinyl bank giveaway item appears to be modeled after the King of Hearts in *Alice in Wonderland*.

BELOW The original International Trade Mart building in New Orleans was built in 1948, and this postcard touted it as "a world market place for wholesale buyers, showing some 700 domestic products as well as the products of 20 foreign countries." As we shall see in a later chapter, the Trade Mart eventually grew up—literally.

As shopping centers gradually came to replace downtowns as retail hubs, their signage had to promote many different businesses all at the same time. With Louisiana's French heritage, it was a foregone conclusion that someone would come up with a Napoleon Plaza, and Metairie certainly did. It appears there were several vacant spots available at the time of this photo. *Debra Jane Seltzer collection.*

One street in West Monroe became known as "Antique Alley" because of all the collectibles stores clustered there. Many of them have now been converted into boutiques, including this one that occupied the street's former Rialto Theater, as seen in 2013. Even with fewer antiques stores, the district is still labeled as such on current maps.

CHAPTER TWO

FRENCH COOKING
(AND OTHER TYPES)

In this chapter, we will be looking at signage connected with food of all types, from restaurants to grocery shelves. In the latter category is the landmark Evangeline Maid bread sign in Lafayette, where the oversized loaf has been revolving for at least six decades or longer. *Stephanie Stuckey collection*.

THIS PAGE The Crystal Preserves billboard in New Orleans stood for nearly sixty years before it, like so many other area landmarks, was severely damaged by Hurricane Katrina in 2005. Fortunately, Preserves was preserved, and a re-creation/reproduction of it was erected atop an apartment building on the site of the old plant. The original version featured steam (generated from the plant's boilers) rising from the chef's pot. *Debra Jane Seltzer collection; Stephanie Stuckey collection.*

Largest Variety of Liquors at Nationally Famous Low Prices

VISIT
THE LARGEST SUPERMARKET
IN THE WORLD

5300 Gentilly Road

Schwegmann's

300 VARIETIES OF CHEESE

GOURMET FOODS, CAMERAS   **FINE WINES and LIQUORS**
AT LOWEST SUPERMARKET PRICES

*Ask any cab driver — he will take you
to the nearest Schwegmann Store.*

TOP Whereas Evangeline Maid is native to Louisiana, Bunny Bread ("That's what Ah said!") hopped out of Illinois into supermarkets nationwide. The bakery in New Orleans stretched this humongous display across the better part of a wall, complete with a version of its traditional blue and white bunny face. *Debra Jane Seltzer collection.*

BOTTOM Now, what about the stores that sold bread, preserves and other food staples? Schwegmann's was the first chain of giant supermarkets in Louisiana, and this New Orleans location on Gentilly Road claimed to be the largest in the world when it opened in 1957. That did not keep the whole chain from going out of business forty years later.

Sometimes the little guys win. Cannata's Supermarket in Morgan City might not have been as huge as Schwegmann's, but it's still in business and Schwegmann's isn't, so there, nyahh. The most interesting thing about Cannata's vintage sign is the panel with the painted lady toting a grocery bag, an element not nearly as common as neon. *Debra Jane Seltzer collection.*

Although not exactly the same as roadside signage, product labels can be considered miniature signs, beckoning to grocery store shoppers instead of automobile travelers. This vintage 1970s display of products from Trappey's certainly shows how varied and colorful the labels for their spices and sauces could be.

THIS PAGE In Phil Harris's theme song "That's What I Like About the South," he refers to "sippin' absinthe in New Orleans," so most likely this famous bar is where he was doing it. These two postcards from about twenty years apart show the evolving styles of signage around the Bourbon Street institution, including its neighbor, the Desire Oyster Bar.

KOLB'S

A Cosmopolitan Restaurant
Catering to all Tastes
St. Charles Near Canal St.

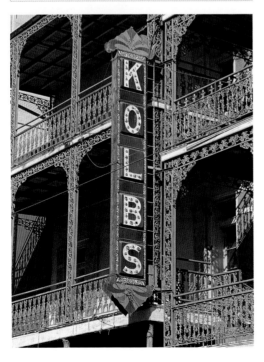

THIS PAGE Kolb's Restaurant bucked the prevailing New Orleans theme of French cooking and dished up German cuisine instead. With its old-world décor covering the interior, Kolb's survived for nearly a century before closing in 1994. Its sign remains on the building as a silent memorial to the once-beloved eatery. *Both, Stephanie Stuckey collection.*

ABOVE New Orleans's Morning Call Coffee Stand began helping denizens of the French Market wake up in 1870. Obviously, its neon coffee cup sign didn't percolate until some time later. Morning Call went into temporary slumber in 2019, but when it reawakened in 2021, it was with a re-creation of this original sign.

OPPOSITE Likely hinting at some ongoing rivalry, the postcards for Café du Monde promoted the establishment as "The Original French Market Coffee Stand." Luckily for us sign enthusiasts, it issued photos showing its red/blue/green display in both daytime and nighttime shots. Café du Monde is still there, but modern-day photos indicate that the neon is not.

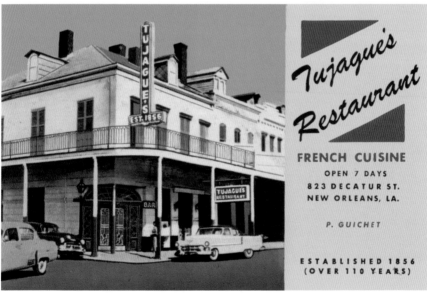

NEW ORLEANS, LA.   HOUSTON, TEX.

OPPOSITE, TOP Despite what the postcard says, the La Louisiane Restaurant did not begin operation in 1835; that was the year its building was constructed as a private residence. The restaurant was actually a product of the 1880s, and this image was a product of 1950. Its many different lives came to an end after Hurricane Katrina in 2005.

OPPOSITE, BOTTOM Tujague's Restaurant can legitimately trace its origins back to 1856, although this postcard view showing its signage was created in 1964. Very little seems to have changed on the outside since then, although turnover in ownership has resulted in modernizing the dining areas.

ABOVE Compared to some of the others, Brennan's Restaurant was a late arrival, not joining the regular pecking order until after World War II. The rooster has consistently been the emblem of Brennan's, prominent in signage and advertising and serving as the mascot for the Roost Bar overlooking the courtyard.

OPPOSITE Just to demonstrate that appearances can be deceiving, this ancient-looking rooftop sign for New Orleans's Palace Café dates back only to that restaurant's founding in 1991. Also notice that while the Palace is owned by a Brennan, it isn't owned by the same Brennan as Brennan's. Clear as gumbo, ain't it? *Stephanie Stuckey collection.*

ABOVE You might have to look closely to see the most notable thing about the Crescent City Steaks sign: the neon detail outlining the eponymous steak at the bottom. Also, pay attention to the neon crescent moon in the center, a symbol of New Orleans and not crescent rolls on the menu. *Debra Jane Seltzer collection.*

BEST STEAKS ON BOURBON STREET
(Most Reasonable Too)
Complete Steak Dinners
From $3.50

A sizzling selection of 6 different cuts to choose from. Also Broiled Lamb Chops and Filet of Trout and our special salad dressings.

Open Every Day
at 5:00 p.m.
to 11:30 p.m.

Complete Cocktail Service

The Embers
STEAK HOUSE

700 Bourbon corner of St. Peter Street 523-1485

Speaking of steak, the name makes it sound like the main meals at the Embers Steak House on Bourbon Street were served well, well, well done. This ad comes to us from 1968; the Embers' flame of life has now gone out, but just when that happened is unclear. Its most recent online reviews—and not good ones, either—are dated 2013.

Steaks were also available, in company with seafood, at the Pearl Restaurant, making New Orleans its oyster since the 1920s. The Pearl clammed up in 2015, but at last report its sign was still hanging on. That could have changed, of course, by the time we went to press. *Stephanie Stuckey collection.*

OPPOSITE Little needs to be said about this, possibly the most famous name in New Orleans restaurants. It did achieve a level of fame unavailable to the others when it was referenced in a classic Bugs Bunny cartoon:
French Chef: Do you mean Antoine of New Orleans?
Bugs: I don't mean Antoine of Flatbush!

ABOVE And speaking of Bugs, in 1949 that scwewy wabbit started hanging out at Da Wabbit Drive-In in Gretna. We wouldn't be surprised if the competing drive-ins in town all got together and sang, "Kill Da Wabbit! Kill Da Wabbit!" *Debra Jane Seltzer collection.*

OPPOSITE, TOP In the days of silent cartoons, there was a popular character named Ko-Ko the Clown, but apparently he had no connection with the Ko-Ko-Mo Drive-In in Bossier City. But don't worry, we'll be running into another famous character later in this chapter when we get to fried chicken places—and you can probably guess who it will be, even with one eye shut. *John Margolies collection.*

OPPOSITE, BOTTOM There isn't much information about the Reed and Bell Drive-In in Alexandria, except that it was part of a chain named after a pair of early A&W Root Beer franchisees. Regardless, prints of this John Margolies photo seem to be available from an amazing number of sources, likely bolstered by the appeal of that neon ice cream cone and root beer mug. *John Margolies collection.*

ABOVE Now let's ramble around Louisiana and rustle up some hamburgers. The Ruston outlet of the small Griff's chain needs a prize for preserving this nostalgic sign; notice the tiny chef at the top, which bears an unmistakable resemblance to the "Speedee" character that once flickered on McDonald's original neon signage.

ABOVE You might have known that we'd somehow end up back on Canal Street again, and in the lower right-hand corner you'll notice the photographer captured the neon sign for a Royal Castle Hamburgers stand ("Fit for a King!"). Royal Castle was a Florida-based entry in the race for small, square burgers pioneered by White Castle and Krystal in other parts of the country.

OPPOSITE, TOP Occasionally, a restaurant will become a turncoat of sorts. It is believed that this Lake Charles restaurant might originally have been a steakhouse, with the descriptive panel later altered to turn it into a burger house. Finally getting out of food service altogether, it became a music house before being destroyed in 2020. *Debra Jane Seltzer collection.*

OPPOSITE, BOTTOM Ted's Frostop Burgers in New Orleans has done a remarkable job of retaining its nostalgic look (not to mention menu) from its beginnings in 1955. And it is proud of that look, too, featuring it prominently on its website. Ted's was "retro" when "retro" still meant "as modern as tomorrow." *Stephanie Stuckey collection.*

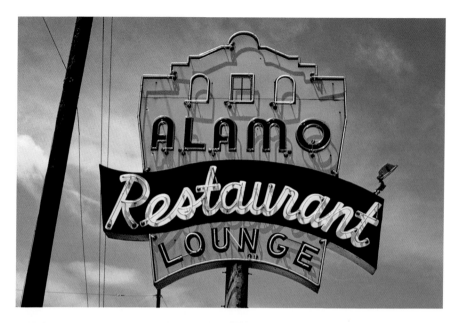

"Known the world over for fine foods!"

OPPOSITE, TOP Remember the Alamo? If you were in Shreveport in the 1960s and 1970s, you probably do—or at least the restaurant that was part of the Alamo Plaza complex on Greenwood Road. We'll be getting around to Shreveport's other two Alamos in our motels chapter a few pages from now. *John Margolies collection.*

OPPOSITE, BOTTOM Like the shot of the Reed and Bell Drive-In included earlier, this John Margolies photo of Shreveport's Sirloin Stockade appears to be one of his most popular ones online. Information about the restaurant itself is harder to find, but it's certain the giant bull in front promised no customers would get a bum steer. An unintentional paradox was Margolies capturing a Piggly Wiggly sign above the steer's back—pork over beef, as it were. *John Margolies collection.*

ABOVE Roussel's Restaurant in LaPlace made sure its sign towered over its surroundings, but the most distinctive thing was its Art Deco building, constructed in 1936 at the height of that design's popularity. Although the restaurant has been closed since 1984, the Roussel's name survives as a LaPlace jewelry store.

ABOVE Like Art Deco in the 1930s, boomerangs became a common design element a couple of decades later. The Revana Restaurant in Bossier City used boomerang shapes to ensure its customers would always come back. *John Margolies collection.*

OPPOSITE These two photos give us a fascinating, if melancholy, glimpse of the changing face of roadside signage. The White Kitchen Restaurant on U.S. 11 at Slidell was thriving when this 1950s postcard view was produced. There was even a notation that its logo of a Native American cooking over a campfire was a registered trademark. But by the time Margolies ran across it circa 1980, the artwork had nearly rusted into obscurity. *Bottom, John Margolies collection.*

ABOVE AND LEFT Southern Maid Donuts have been a Shreveport institution since 1937; this impressive signage can be seen at their store at the intersection of I-20 and U.S. 171. In the 1950s, Southern Maid was a sponsor of the *Louisiana Hayride* radio show, and the company loves to point out that their jingle was the only commercial ever performed by then-series-regular Elvis Presley in 1954. *Both, Stephanie Stuckey collection; photos by Holly Aguirre.*

OPPOSITE, TOP While we're on the subject of sponsors, let's see how some companies worked their signage into those beloved local kids' TV shows of the 1950s and 1960s. Here, Al Bolton wrangles up some Hostess snack cakes in what appears to be a grocery store display on the set of his *Al's Corral* show on KSLA-TV in Shreveport.

OPPOSITE, BOTTOM Meanwhile, on KPLC-TV in Lake Charles, gentle Jeb Roberts entertained area kids on *Kartoon Kapers*. For this promotional shot, we get not only the show's backdrop signage and one of the KPLC cameras but also Ms. Roberts advertising sponsor Jack's Cookies.

ABOVE It isn't known whether Gambino's Bakery in Metairie ever advertised on a TV show, children's or otherwise, but after paying for this sign with its plethora of detail in the icing, flowers and candles, they might not have had enough money left over for TV commercials. The sign is believed to date from 1949, the year after Louisiana got its first TV station. *Debra Jane Seltzer collection.*

OPPOSITE, TOP Likely many of Gambino's birthday cakes were served with Coca-Cola to drink. Sign historian Debra Jane Seltzer's research shows that this neon masterpiece in Baton Rouge was created sometime between 1946 and 1960 (accounts and memories differ). She reports that because its delicate neon tubes are particularly vulnerable to hurricane damage, it has been refurbished at least three times (circa 1985, 2002 and 2014). *Debra Jane Seltzer collection.*

OPPOSITE, BOTTOM We'll finish up our food chapter with a brief look at some relics of chain restaurants. Borden's once had ice cream parlors in conjunction with its dairy plants nationwide, but this one in Lafayette is believed to be the only remaining example. Elsie the Cow, Elmer the Bull and the rest of their herd obviously found Louisiana to be prime grazing. *Stephanie Stuckey collection.*

STEAK . . . AT HAMBURGER PRICES

BONANZA SIRLOIN PIT #146
131 St. Charles Ave.

BONANZA SIRLOIN PIT #141
59 Westbank Expwy.

BONANZA SIRLOIN PIT #144
4517 Veterans Blvd.

OPEN DAILY 11 a.m.-10 p.m.
Fridays 11 a.m.-12 midnight
Saturdays 11 a.m.-1 a.m.

TOP In the 1950s and 1960s, fast-food outlets latched onto the value of distinctive buildings that could serve as additional forms of signage. Kentucky Fried Chicken's pagoda-roofed structures with red and white stripes and a cupola topped with a Colonel Sanders weathervane were so distinctive that they are easily identifiable even in a reconditioned form. This rather sad example was in Bossier City. *Debra Jane Seltzer collection.*

BOTTOM The chain of Bonanza Sirloin Pits was inspired by NBC's hit TV series in the early 1960s. By the time of this 1971 ad, its three locations in New Orleans showed that not everyone in that city was eating at Antoine's or La Louisiane.

66

During a 1960s craze for naming fast-food chains after celebrities, singing cowboy Roy Rogers loaned his moniker to a string of roast beef restaurants. This incredible example of their neon chuck wagon sign was still hitting the happy trails in New Orleans circa 1980. And since we have already referenced the Frostop Root Beer chain, notice one of its giant mugs in the lower right-hand corner. *John Margolies collection.*

ABOVE If you choose to believe the official company line of today, New Orleans–based Popeyes Famous Fried Chicken was named after *French Connection* character Popeye Doyle and not Popeye the Sailor Man. That certainly did not prevent the chicken chain from using the squinty sailor in all of its advertising and interior decoration—although not on its exterior signage—for some forty years (and even in animated TV commercials in which Popeye rasps, "They named it after me!"). Popeye Doyle is nowhere to be seen in this 1979 giveaway calendar.

OPPOSITE Another chain with disputed origins for its name was Lums, whose location in Baton Rouge was the subject of this ad. The company denied that it was named for the classic *Lum and Abner* radio comedy series of the 1930s and 1940s, yet it did attempt to open a chain of Abner's Beef Houses, which somewhat negated that claim. Lums was famed for its "hot dogs steamed in beer" and certainly played up the beer angle even further here.

CHAPTER THREE
KEEP 'EM ROLLING

In the next few pages, we'll pay a brief visit to signage relating to transportation—automobile and otherwise. And your eyes don't deceive you; we're back on Canal Street once more, only this time you should be paying attention to that Chevrolet billboard and the Ford billboard a little farther distant. And since we're talking about transportation, notice the Jet Delta sign on the right-hand side.

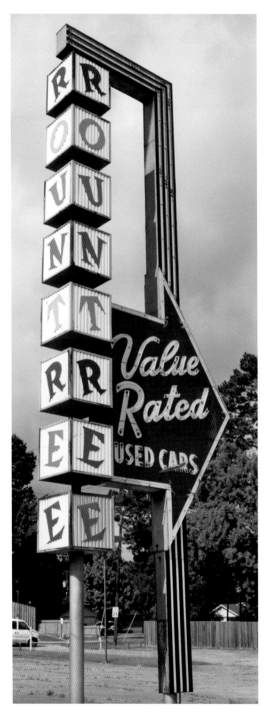

OPPOSITE, TOP Perhaps you recall the Lincoln-Mercury signage of the early 1970s, usually depicted in ads with a snarling mountain lion perched atop. (Some signs and billboards used artwork of a cougar to complete the picture.) Obviously this dealership's sign in Metairie predated the lion, but its design is certainly representative of an earlier time. *Debra Jane Seltzer collection.*

OPPOSITE, BOTTOM Hopefully John Margolies was not in need of Jim's Wheel Alignment services when he stumbled across this relic in Baton Rouge. It looked like the neon needed more work than any of the customers' wheels. *John Margolies collection.*

LEFT Used car dealerships often had more eye-catching signs than new car dealerships, due to the need for standing out from the competition. Rountree Used Cars in Shreveport spelled out its name in multicolored ABC blocks, presumed to rotate at some point in its career. *Debra Jane Seltzer collection.*

OPPOSITE Just what was a "motor exchange," anyway? Whatever its purpose, this beauty in Baton Rouge would be worth studying just to see the detail in that neon engine block at the top. *Debra Jane Seltzer collection.*

ABOVE If Burger King sells hamburgers, would Auto King in Plaquemine sell autos? Not quite, but it seems one might get a whopper of a deal on mufflers if the place were still in business—which it isn't. *Debra Jane Seltzer collection.*

OPPOSITE, TOP Debra Jane Seltzer's research indicated that this combination auto repair/auto storage outfit was established in 1957. No reason to doubt that, but this sign sure looks more like something that would have been contemporary with the Model A Ford. Just shows what a hard life in the outdoors can do, I suppose. *Debra Jane Seltzer collection.*

OPPOSITE, BOTTOM With that giant clock, Baton Rouge's Margo Trucking drivers didn't have to guess whether they were on schedule. As a bonus, we get a pair of late 1970s/ early 1980s billboards, including Virginia Slims cigarettes (of "You've come a long way, baby" fame). *John Margolies collection.*

ABOVE It would appear that Kelly's Million Dollar Truck Terminal in Minden (thirty-one miles ahead, according to the faded lettering) was spending considerably less than that on maintenance of this eye-catching billboard by the time this photo was taken. Although almost rusted into obscurity, it seems Union Oil was the sponsor of choice. *John Margolies collection.*

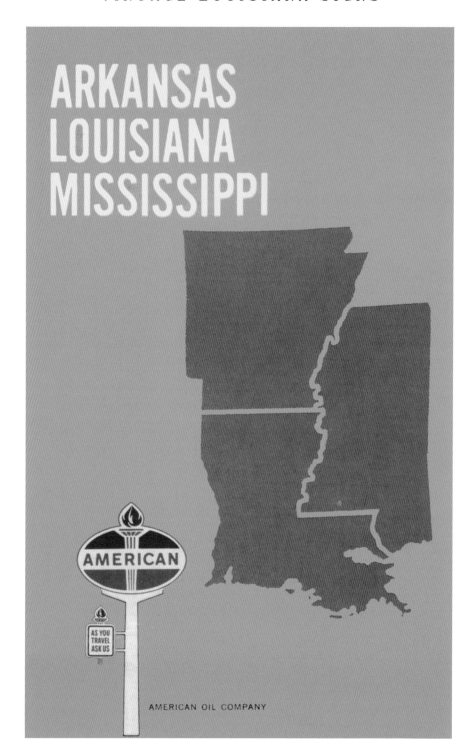

OPPOSITE The "torch and oval" sign represented different gasoline brands at different times in various parts of the country, but by the late 1960s, it had come to be the emblem of American Oil. During the next decade, it would be further simplified, and the colors adjusted, to become Amoco.

ABOVE Sinclair had used dinosaurs in its advertising since the 1930s, to hammer home the age of its crude oils, but it was 1959 before this familiar logo was introduced. Some signs were flat porcelain enamel, illuminated by floodlights, but this was one of the higher-grade models. The flashing red light at the top was non-typical, however. *John Margolies collection.*

CHAPTER FOUR

LULLABY AND GOOD NIGHT

Now, let's take a breather and find a good place to stay for the night before continuing our journey. We'll be looking over lodging that ranges from downtown hotels to roadside motels, and this example seems to be a bit of both. At far right, notice the really odd sign that even felt compelled to spell out its Tamanaca name in two-letter syllables. Among the amenities listed on the back is "free ice cubes." Cool!

Now, this is what most people think of as a downtown hotel. The Roosevelt is still there and more elegant than ever, now a part of the prestigious Waldorf Astoria company.

Another downtown New Orleans hotel, the Monteleone, opened in 1886, but since neon signs hadn't been invented yet, it had to wait some sixty years before it got this one. The sign has been renovated since this photo was made, but so faithfully that it really looks about the same. *Debra Jane Seltzer collection.*

Now, what better name could you find for a New Orleans motel than the Mardi Gras Courts? This would have catered to automobile tourists more so than the high and mighty downtown hotels. *John Margolies collection.*

U. S. HIGHWAY 11 & 90 EAST, NEW ORLEANS 22, LA.

ABOVE AND OPPOSITE It has been stated that the whole idea of being on vacation is to feel like you're somewhere else when you're already somewhere else. Perhaps not intentionally, both of these New Orleans motels chose names and signage that had a strong flavor of their relatives in the far-off fairyland of Florida. *Above, Debra Jane Seltzer collection.*

Now, here's an unusually colorful New Orleans motel, but the message on the back has historical significance: "Spent the weekend with Tom and then came here—Could enjoy it more if the news sounded better." The postmark? October 28, 1962, during the Cuban missile crisis that had Americans wondering if they would wake up in the morning—whether at home or in a motel.

THIS PAGE Both of these motels could be found on U.S. 90 east of New Orleans, and they had something else in common. Although their signs didn't show up in their postcard photos, each was proud enough of its neon creation to picture it as an added graphic. The Cedar Park Court took out extra insurance to be sure travelers would notice it by installing a lighted beacon at the very apex of its sign.

Sometimes appearances can be deceiving. At the time of this photo, it looked like the London Lodge was falling down, but the condition of its sign was due to recent Hurricane Katrina damage. Despite all setbacks, as of this writing it soldiers on like a grenadier outside Buckingham Palace. *Debra Jane Seltzer collection.*

THIS PAGE We haven't made it out of New Orleans yet, but these two roadside motels took differing approaches to attracting customers. The Sherwood, on U.S. 51, advertised that sightseeing tours left the motel three times daily. The Rustic Lodge, on U.S. 90, also advertised tours but contradicted its own name by mentioning its location in a suburban shopping area. Maybe it was more rustic once upon a time.

THIS PAGE It appears the Roto-Sphere salesman in Bossier City made a sale at both of these local motels. We have to wonder whether he promised each of them that they'd have the only Roto-Sphere in town. The Colonial Inn decided to augment theirs with that popular boomerang shape. *Both, John Margolies collection.*

THIS PAGE In nearby Shreveport, these signs certainly illustrate two different eras. The Palomar's is a patchwork quilt combining the days when "air conditioning" was a selling point and a later time when "color TV" was still a novelty. Then we have the Town and Country, which looks something like an upscale lounge, with a sign that was probably larger than an entire room at the Palomar. *Top, Debra Jane Seltzer collection.*

OPPOSITE Ten Flags Over Louisiana? No, Baton Rouge didn't feature a theme park by that name, but it did have a motel. (The real Six Flags would eventually have a very brief and stormy stay in New Orleans, but we'll get to that story in our final chapter.) *Debra Jane Seltzer collection.*

THIS PAGE Elsewhere in Baton Rouge, the Shades Motel employed the tradition of illustrating its pool with waving bathing beauties; the Colonial Court in Alexandria was recommended by Duncan Hines in the days when he was a real live travel writer and not a brand name for packaged cake mix. *Both, Al Coleman collection.*

It's lucky for us all that Margolies happened across this almost-decayed relic circa 1980. The location is unknown, but we can deduce that it was somewhere south of Homer. Sights like this are virtually extinct along the ever-changing roadside of the twenty-first century. *John Margolies collection.*

OPPOSITE, TOP Shure, an' ye'll be feelin' like you've found yer pot o' gold at the end o' the rainbow if ye rest yer weary bones at the Shamrock Motor Inn in Vidalia. Recommended by leprechauns instead of Duncan Hines, the Shamrock barely qualifies for this book, as it was only one mile from downtown Natchez, Mississippi.

OPPOSITE, BOTTOM The long, slow changeover from independent motels to chains began in the 1930s and 1940s when various associations were formed to give travelers some sort of assurance that a motel that displayed their emblem met quality standards. United Hotel Courts was one of these; this postcard appears to be generic, but the info on the back gives its location as twenty minutes east of New Orleans on U.S. 11 and U.S. 90.

ABOVE Imperial 400 was a California-based chain that staked a claim in Lake Charles. Its locations were marked by a gull-wing shape to the main office, as seen at far left. The mascot was a cartoon king in Scottish garb, proclaiming, "Aye, Royal Accommodations and Thr-riffty Rates." *Al Coleman collection.*

The Alamo Plaza chain, with its otherwise nondescript buildings fronted by facades shaped like the famous San Antonio landmark, had several locations around Shreveport. This was one of the earlier styles, as seen in the late 1970s. *John Margolies collection.*

The Grand Plaza in Lake Charles appears to have been either an Alamo Plaza that turned traitor or a motel that just didn't care about flaunting trademark law. Either way, this postcard was mailed in March 1952, at which time the genuine Alamo Plaza chain was still holding down the fort in many southern and midwestern cities.

We don't even need to point out that the most famous motel chain of all was Holiday Inn. This one in Alexandria was among its earliest locations in Louisiana; at far right, notice that the iconic "Great Sign" still bore the HOTEL designation for the benefit of those who were not yet familiar with the brand. The chartreuse roof was another characteristic of the early Holiday Inns.

By the time my family and I stayed at this Holiday Inn on U.S. 90 east of New Orleans in July 1969, the Great Sign and the rest of the architecture had settled into the form with which most travelers of that era would be familiar. Google shows only some office buildings occupying this address today.

TOP Also during the 1960s, many Holiday Inns supplemented their giant roadside sign with this version, which consisted of backlit lettering against a large brick wall. This was how it looked in Lake Charles.

BOTTOM What makes this nighttime shot any different from the others? In 1982, Holiday Inn announced that it would be phasing out the flashing Great Signs and replacing them with a more "modernized" logo that was not so expensive to maintain. When I stayed at the one in Slidell in February 1984, on the trip mentioned in the introduction, I was surprised that its Great Sign was still blinking as colorfully as ever and felt this would probably be the last opportunity I would have to see one. I was right.

Signs that emulated the look of Holiday Inns without being direct copies of them were fairly common. The Jo-Dan Motel in Shreveport did not completely ape the Holiday Inn look, but that neon star with radiating neon beams at the top wasn't exactly an original creation by the signmaker, either. *John Margolies collection.*

As the name suggested, the chain of Downtowner Motor Inns was built near main business districts rather than out on the open roads where tourists would be passing by. This 1968 ad for the Downtowner in New Orleans put more emphasis on the attractive ladies in its Cabaret Toulouse than on the motel amenities.

TOP TraveLodge's Sleepy Bear was "bearly" visible on the Alexandria motel's sign above the roofline from the angle of this 1968 postcard. The custom of having motel room doors painted in multicolored hues is one that we do not see very often anymore.

BOTTOM Ramada Inn's portly, balding butler was officially known as Uncle Ben. He most often appeared in the form you see here, with his blue tailcoat and top hat and red knee breeches. This was the Ramada at the New Orleans airport but technically located in the suburb of Kenner.

OPPOSITE, TOP Beginning in 1961, the Admiral Benbow Inns—named for a hostelry in the *Treasure Island* novel—tried to navigate the seven seas of roadside motels, but the chain crested in the mid-1970s before sinking in the drink. This view of the Benbow on U.S. 80 in Monroe at least gave men and women equal space in the obligatory pool shot.

OPPOSITE, BOTTOM Using an entire wall as supplemental signage was uncommon. This Econo Lodge, found somewhere in Louisiana in 1984, continued its Scottish plaid pattern to the wall above and behind the main office, extending the logo that also appeared on the plastic roadside sign.

ABOVE Budget chain Motel 6 took its name from the original $6.60-per-night room rate. This Shreveport Motel 6 displays the early version of the logo on its sign, with the giant orange 6 and aqua-colored MOTEL—just about the only colorful things about the deliberately bland and no-frills appearance of the rest of the property.

CHAPTER FIVE

HOW TO ATTRACT
THE TOURISTS

Louisiana's tourism industry was a bit different (and nowhere near as flashy) than states such as Florida and Tennessee, but it had a flavor all its own. This postcard collage was meant to promote the not-so-family-friendly appeal of Bourbon Street, cramming as many of that district's signs as possible into a single image.

TOP You have to give Bourbon Street credit: it never pretended to be something it wasn't. This 1963 postcard showing some of its more subdued signage was captioned "Crazy Mixed-Up Bourbon Street" and claimed, "It is jumping from dusk to dawn with Dixieland jazz and girlie floor shows." As we shall see in our next chapter, the floor wasn't all that was showing, girlies.

BOTTOM Maybe Pirate's Alley didn't have much to offer in the way of signage, but those hand-painted portraits served much the same purpose. So did those pink-and-aqua storefronts.

106

TOP From what we have seen so far, it may be obvious that Louisiana didn't expend a lot of effort on tourism that would appeal to the kids in the family. One attraction that did court the kiddie trade was Shreveport's Children's Zoo in Ford Park, the entrance gate of which is seen here in 1957. Ford Park is still there, but the zoo is not.

BOTTOM A children's attraction that does still exist is New Orleans's Storyland, an important throwback to the days of baby boom tourism. This early postcard shows the original alphabet blocks entrance signage; the Old Woman in the Shoe display is still around, although it is now painted somewhat more colorfully than in the 1950s.

VISIT
YOGI BEAR'S

JELLYSTONE PARK
CAMP-RESORT

IN
ROBERT
LOUISIANA

THIS PAGE The extant chain of Yogi Bear's Jellystone Park Campgrounds has come and gone from Louisiana's highways more than once. This brochure from the campground in Robert dates from the early 1980s. The "welcome" sign was at a Jellystone in Calhoun in 2013 that has now taken its pic-a-nic basket and scrammed.

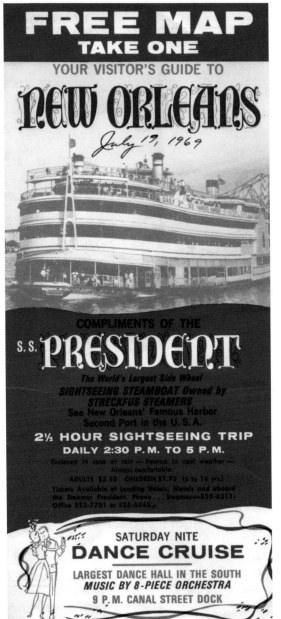

FREE MAP
TAKE ONE
YOUR VISITOR'S GUIDE TO

New Orleans

July 19, 1969

COMPLIMENTS OF THE
S.S. PRESIDENT

The World's Largest Side Wheel
SIGHTSEEING STEAMBOAT *Owned by*
STRECKFUS STEAMERS
See New Orleans' Famous Harbor
Second Port in the U.S.A.

2½ HOUR SIGHTSEEING TRIP
DAILY 2:30 P.M. TO 5 P.M.

Enclosed in case of rain — Heated in cool weather —
Always comfortable.
ADULTS $3.50 CHILDREN $1.75 (6 to 16 yrs.)
Tickets Available at Leading Hotels, Motels and aboard
the Steamer President. Phone . . . Steamer—525-6311;
Office 523-7701 or 525-6545.

SATURDAY NITE
DANCE CRUISE
LARGEST DANCE HALL IN THE SOUTH
MUSIC BY 8-PIECE ORCHESTRA
9 P.M. CANAL STREET DOCK

ABOVE Since the Lake Pontchartrain Causeway is a nearly twenty-four-mile-long bridge, naturally it did not have billboards or other types of advertising during that stretch. But this was how the tollbooths at one end or the other appeared shortly after its opening in 1956; today, the tolls are collected only for southbound traffic.

LEFT Maybe it isn't exactly signage, but that's a great logo for the sidewheel steamboat *President* that offered cruises on the Mississippi from the early 1940s to the late 1980s. As you can see from the handwritten date on this brochure, this was one of the sights my family saw on our July 1969 visit to New Orleans. Perhaps because there was nothing about the *President* that would appeal to a six-year-old, I have zero memory of us ever taking this cruise— if, indeed, we ever did.

Another sternwheeler that plied the waterways around New Orleans was the *Cotton Blossom*, but instead of the Mississippi, it journeyed into the bayou country. As this postcard view indicates, it was popular enough to crowd lots of tourists onto its multiple decks.

Historians still debate whether Jim Bowie ever spent any time in Opelousas in general, or this house in particular, during his time living in Louisiana. Regardless, the house and its neighboring Jim Bowie Oak brought what tourism they could to the small town. For our purposes, just as notable is the glowing neon sign for the Palace Café next door; it is somewhat surprising that the owners didn't succumb to Bowie-mania and call it the Alamo Café.

THIS PAGE What more typically southern roadside attraction could there be but a snake farm? John Margolies did not record exactly where he found these billboards, but most likely they were on U.S. 61 either north or south of LaPlace. While snakes are certainly common in the Louisiana bayous, cobras and boa constrictors are not typically a part of the crowd. *Both, John Margolies collection.*

THIS PAGE, TOP Wherever there are tourists, there must be gift shops to help them unload some of their cash. Su-San Gifts, on U.S. 80 at Shreveport, was a little different than most in that it also promoted its collection of live parakeets, finches and canaries and the supplies to keep them happy and tweeting.

OPPOSITE, BOTTOM Those past a certain age may recall when roadside parks with concrete picnic tables were a staple of any road trip. This photo from a 1950s Louisiana tourist guide captures the charming localized signage that prompted drivers to pull over for a spell.

THIS PAGE If you are a small town with a rather unusual name, how can you put that to work in the lucrative tourist trade? If you're New Iberia, you fashion an elaborate neon sign with literary icon Evangeline, apparently loafing from her day job of making bread in Lafayette; if you're Transylvania, you go right for the jugular in a Count Dracula vein.

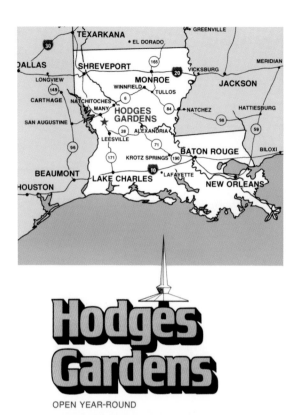

Hodges Gardens

OPEN YEAR-ROUND

OPPOSITE Earlier, we mentioned the roadside staple of snake farms; another sight that could be counted on in any tourist area was a wax museum. While this postcard view was meant to illustrate New Orleans's St. Louis Cathedral, the photographer captured an advertisement for the Musee Conti Museum of Wax on the back of a touring buggy. If Dracula got tired of hanging around in Transylvania, he could probably have made a second home at the Haunted Dungeon.

THIS PAGE These images seem to hint there were ambitions for Hodges Gardens to become Louisiana's parallel to Florida's Cypress Gardens. The acreage never attained that sort of legendary status but did grow to include an observation tower (seen as part of the logo) and its own motel and restaurant. It became a state park in 2007 and closed permanently eleven years later.

CHAPTER SIX

WE'LL HAVE BIG FUN
ON THE BAYOU

We kick off our chapter on various forms of amusements by going to the movies—and your eyes don't deceive you; we're back on Canal Street again. This image likely dates from 1931, judging from the movies advertised on the marquees, and also because the Loew's State and Saenger Theaters appear to still be using incandescent bulbs in their signs rather than neon.

OPPOSITE This different angle of the same area comes from a decade later, and changes are abundant. Loew's has a completely different style sign; it's hard to say for sure about the Saenger, but it appears to have traded in its screw-in bulb lettering. Look closely to see other landmarks, such as a Woolworth's and the Maison Blanche store towering above the street.

ABOVE As we all know, not everyone was welcome in all the downtown theaters. Therefore, New Orleans's Carver Theater opened in 1950 to serve the underserved African American population. After some rough years, especially after Hurricane Katrina, it was reopened in 2014. *Debra Jane Seltzer collection.*

In Shreveport, the most justifiably famous of movie palaces is the Strand. When John Margolies visited it around 1980, the long process of bringing it back from the dead was just beginning. The ultimate renovation did not include this sign, which now resides in an exhibit in Las Vegas. *John Margolies collection.*

LEFT The Sabine Theater in the small town of Many is most surely named after the river that flows through parts of western Louisiana and eastern Texas. A few miles south of Many was the site of the Hodges Gardens attraction, with which we closed out the previous chapter. *Debra Jane Seltzer collection.*

RIGHT Movie producer Joy N. Houck Sr. built a string of theaters across Louisiana, Texas and Mississippi and named them after himself. New Orleans was his home base, and this was how that city's Joy Theater appeared in the late 1970s. Occasionally, decaying remnants of other Joy locations can be spotted in various small towns. *John Margolies collection.*

ABOVE It might seem the Dixie Theater in Ruston would date from the same segregation period as the Carver in New Orleans, but oddly, the theater did not receive that name until 2006, after a renovation program. Prior to that, it enjoyed several other identities; it was called the Rialto during the 1950s, when the clone of the Holiday Inn star was added to the marquee. *Debra Jane Seltzer collection.*

OPPOSITE In New Iberia, the Evangeline Theater carries on the theme we saw in the town's welcome sign in the previous chapter. This version of the theater sign dates back to 1939; it has since been renovated with LED bulbs replacing the original style seen here. *John Margolies collection.*

ABOVE AND OPPOSITE Naturally, nightclubs were a big part of Bourbon Street's entertainment scene, especially when visitors could see such jazz legends as trumpeter Al Hirt and clarinetist Pete Fountain in person. This Fountain postcard was postmarked in October 1973 and mailed to Old San Juan, Puerto Rico; the writer commented, "New Orleans is quite a place, old and quaint." Coming from Old San Juan, that must have been quite a compliment.

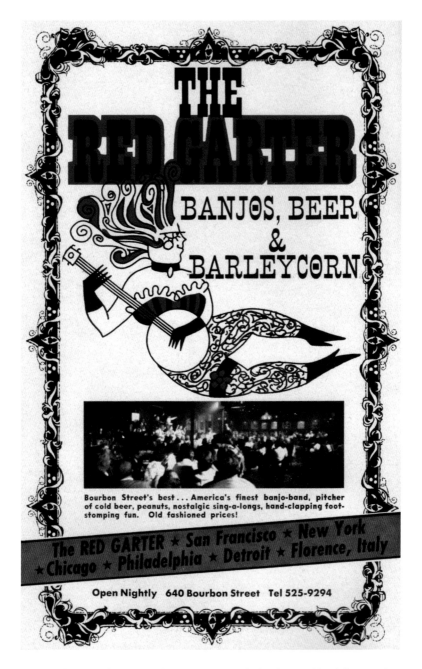

As we said earlier, Bourbon Street has never pretended to be anything it isn't, and these next few night spots will prove it. The Red Garter summed up most of the neighborhood's appeal with "banjos, beer and barleycorn," but unlike most of the district's businesses, it had other locations from coast to coast.

TOP Places like the Sho-Bar and 500 Club could technically have been included in our restaurants chapter, but ads such as these are a good indication that people were not primarily visiting them because of the food's reputation. The logos from their signage were reproduced in the ads, but likely few patrons were paying any attention to those, either.

BOTTOM This April 1967 ad for Bourbon Street's Lido is fascinating for its place in entertainment history. The "adults only" marionette show *Les Poupées de Paris* had been touring the country for several years, but two months after this ad, nightclub puppeteers Sid and Marty Krofft would open a more family-friendly puppet theater at Six Flags Over Georgia—and then, in 1969, would complete their transition into legendary children's producers with their *H.R. Pufnstuf* TV series.

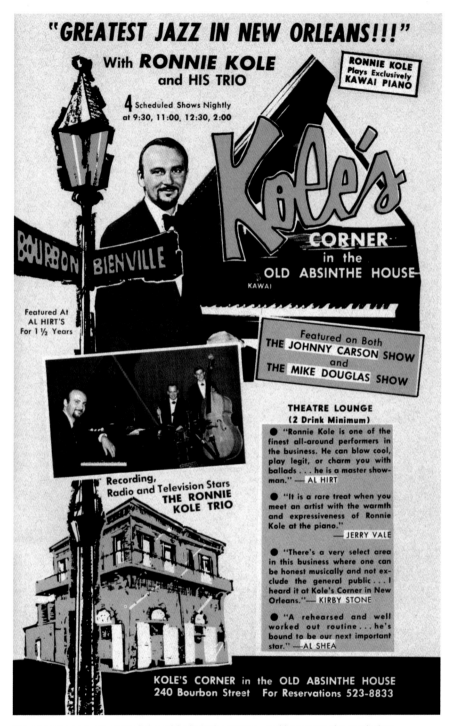

Many pages ago, we visited the Old Absinthe House, and here was the act being presented there in 1968. Kole's Corner, at least, put the emphasis on jazz and not nudes (puppet or flesh-and-blood).

TOP No, this isn't the more famous South of the Border tourist trap; we will have to wait until we do *Vintage South Carolina Signs* to get that story. But this lounge got its name for a very similar reason: it was in St. Francisville, just south of the Mississippi/Louisiana border. It has been guarding that border since 1947. *Debra Jane Seltzer collection.*

BOTTOM With a sign looking like something from the Las Vegas Strip, the Saddle and Spur Lounge rounded up any strays looking for night life in Monroe. Obviously, jazz was not the only type of music favored by Louisiana residents. *John Margolies collection.*

ABOVE In contrast to nightclubs and girlie shows, some folks get their jollies from sports. Tulane Stadium became famous as the home of the annual Sugar Bowl after that contest was inaugurated in 1935. Most likely the Sugar Bowl signage on the field in this postcard is artistic license, although it may be meant to represent band members spelling out the name.

LEFT Tulane Stadium was effectively replaced by the Louisiana Superdome when that mega-facility opened in 1975. This postcard view probably dates from that period, and that scrolling sign is certainly a product of its time. The Superdome, of course, made a different kind of history when it was used for Hurricane Katrina refugees in 2005.

Yes, there are sports other than football. Bowling alleys became immensely popular in the decade following World War II. The Rock 'n' Bowl in Lafayette isn't quite that old—in fact, its signage might be considered part of the trend toward the "retro" look, or trying to appear older than it really is. It's still an impressive sight. *Stephanie Stuckey collection.*

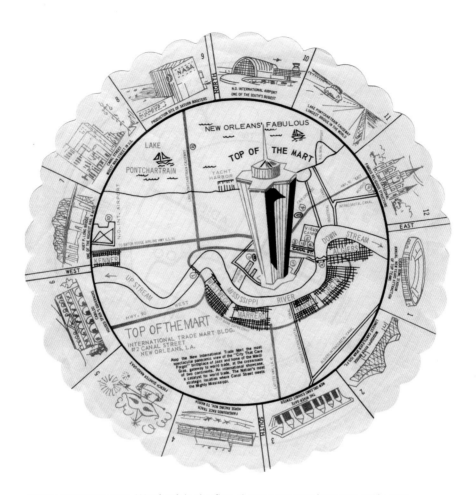

ABOVE AND OPPOSITE Way back in the first chapter, we saw how New Orleans's International Trade Mart got started. By 1965, the complex had moved to a new location and drew attention with its Top of the Mart Lounge that actually revolved atop the thirty-three-story building. The entire complex closed in 2011, and the revolving lounge's dizzying three-feet-per-minute spin came to a halt.

TOP Long before people were taking a ride on Top of the Mart, they were enjoying the sights at Pontchartrain Beach Amusement Park. The funhouse in this postcard had gone through several different names, but the giant grinning clown head at far right was the very emblem of Pontchartrain Beach, even more recognizable than any signage.

BOTTOM The Pontchartrain Beach park dated to 1928, but this postcard view was made some thirty years later. By 1958, the signage for the rides and other attractions had evolved into a colorful cornucopia of what would now be termed "mid-century modern." Back then, it was just called "fun."

In 1952, the park's other attractions gained a companion in the Bali Ha'i tiki bar and lounge, obviously appealing to the adults who brought their kids to Pontchartrain Beach. This ad appeared in 1961, demonstrating the wide appeal of the park's features to all ages.

ABOVE AND OPPOSITE The late 1950s saw the blooming of the dinosaur-and-windmill style of miniature golf courses. Pontchartrain Beach's Around the World in 18 Holes course might not have included dinosaurs, but it had a windmill and other obstacles representing various foreign lands. Naturally, the globe that served as an identifying sign rotated.

Pontchartrain Beach closed after the 1983 operating season, leaving fifty-five years of fond memories as a memorial. The rest of New Orleans's amusement park history seems to have been cursed. For example, Jazzland opened in time for the summer of 2000 but had to declare bankruptcy only two years later.

In 2003, the ex-Jazzland reopened as Six Flags New Orleans. As the logo from its souvenir map shows, by that time the Six Flags chain had long since abandoned its original concept of being based on the six different nations' flags that had flown over a particular area (Texas, Georgia, Mid-America). Now the Six Flags logo was simply six multicolored pennants with no connection to history.

We'll never know whether Six Flags New Orleans would have lasted any longer than Jazzland. Two years after it opened, it closed just before Hurricane Katrina stormed ashore, and that was the end of its story. In the twenty years since, probably more people have trespassed to see its ruins than ever visited while the park was open, and this sign became something of a tombstone for the doomed park.

ABOVE We can't leave Louisiana without one more visit to Canal Street, this time in 1958. There seems to be a difference of opinion regarding the purpose of those electric fleur-de-lis emblems on every lamppost; they could possibly be Christmas decorations, but some believe they could have been part of the Mardi Gras décor.

OPPOSITE, TOP The City Putt miniature golf course in New Orleans fills in the gap that was never filled by Six Flags, in that its obstacles represent different aspects of Louisiana history. And what would any such collection be without our old yuletide buddy Mr. Bingle? *Debra Jane Seltzer collection.*

OPPOSITE, BOTTOM Natchitoches went all out to supplement its usual lighted nighttime signs with a plethora of Christmas decorations each year. So, with a view like this and Mr. Bingle still on duty in New Orleans, what else can we say but, "Merry Christmas to all, and to all a good night"?

CHRISTMAS FESTIVAL—NATCHITOCHES, LOUISIANA